ICONS

JAPAN STYLE

JAPAN

Exteriors   Interiors

STYLE

Details

PHOTOS: **Reto Guntli**
EDITOR **Angelika Taschen**

TASCHEN

HONG KONG KÖLN LONDON LOS ANGELES MADRID PARIS TOKYO

Front Cover: *Kaiseki* several-course dinner at Yoshida Sanso, Kyoto.
Couverture: Le raffinement d'un dîner *kaiseki* à Yoshida Sanso, Kyoto.
Umschlagvorderseite: Ein mehrgängiges *kaiseki*-Mahl im Gästehaus Yoshida Sanso, Kyoto.

Back Cover: Bedroom at Nishirokkaku-cho, an 1880s Kyoto townhouse *(machiya)*.
Dos de couverture: Une pièce préparée pour la nuit dans Nishirokkaku-cho, une maison de ville *(machiya)* de Kyoto datant des années 1880.
Umschlagrückseite: Schlafzimmer im Nishirokkaku-cho, einem restaurierten Stadthaus *(machiya)* in Kyoto aus den 1880er-Jahren.

© 2008 TASCHEN GmbH
Hohenzollernring 53, D–50672 Köln
www.taschen.com

Concept, layout and editing by Angelika Taschen, Berlin
General project management by Stephanie Bischoff, Cologne
Texts by Daisann McLane, Hong Kong
Lithography by Thomas Grell, Cologne
German translation by Ingrid Hacker-Klier, Hebertsfelden
French translation by Philippe Safavi, Paris

Printed in Italy
ISBN 978-3-8365-0483-6

CONTENTS SOMMAIRE INHALT

Living "green" is the buzzword these days for architects and designers, from Los Angeles to London. But in Japan, "green" is an old tradition. Japanese houses have been built to conserve energy and resources, and to harmonize with nature, for more than 500 years. The simplicity, functionality, and minimalism of Japanese style inspired Western architects like Frank Lloyd Wright at the beginning of the 20th century. The homes and spaces in this book inspire us to consider new ways of living as we enter this century.

Is it possible to live a modern life in harmony with the natural world? The Japanese homes in the following pages present a panorama of possibilities. Inside the *machiya*, Kyoto's 19th-century urban townhouses, natural sunlight, handmade bamboo shades, and *shoji* paper screens create the illusion of outdoor living in long, narrow city buildings. The mists of autumn shroud the thatched roofs of writer Alex Kerr's 200-year-old Japanese farmhouse, which gets its heating from wood-burning hearths recessed into the floors.

DESIGN AS GREEN AS THE TEA

De Los Angeles à Londres, les architectes et les designers ne parlent que du retour à la nature. Toutefois, au Japon, l'écologie est une tradition ancienne. Depuis plus de 500 ans, les maisons nippones sont conçues pour conserver l'énergie, préserver les ressources naturelles et s'harmoniser avec leur environnement. Dès le début du 20ᵉ siècle, leur simplicité, leur fonctionnalité et leur minimalisme ont inspiré des architectes occidentaux comme Frank Lloyd Wright. Les demeures et les espaces inclus dans cet ouvrage nous invitent à réfléchir à de nouvelles manières de vivre en ce début de siècle.

Peut-on mener une vie moderne en harmonie avec le monde naturel ? Les maisons japonaises présentées au fil des pages qui suivent présentent tout un éventail de possibilités. Dans les machiya *du 19ᵉ siècle, ces longues maisons étroites de Kyoto, la lumière naturelle, les stores en bambou et les* shôji *– des écrans en papier – créent l'illusion de vivre à l'extérieur. La ferme vieille de 200 ans où vit l'auteur Alex Kerr, dont les toits en chaume se perdent dans les brumes d'automne, est chauffée par des foyers en terre creusés à même le sol. Les « cinq éléments », composants essentiels de l'architecture*

»Grün« zu bauen und zu wohnen ist heute zum Schlagwort für Architekten und Designer von Los Angeles bis London geworden. Doch in Japan hat die »grüne« Philosophie eine uralte Tradition. Seit über 500 Jahren waren japanische Häuser darauf ausgerichtet, Energie zu sparen, Ressourcen zu schonen und mit der Natur zu harmonieren. Die Schlichtheit, Funktionalität und der Minimalismus des japanischen Stils wirkten Anfang des letzten Jahrhunderts inspirierend auf westliche Architekten wie Frank Lloyd Wright. Und auch heute, zu Beginn unseres Jahrhunderts, lassen wir uns durch Wohnhäuser und Interieurs, wie sie in diesem Buch gezeigt werden, dazu anregen, neue Wege der Gestaltung einzuschlagen.

Ist es möglich, ein modernes Leben im Einklang mit der Natur zu führen? Die japanischen Häuser präsentieren auf den folgenden Seiten ein weites Panorama von Möglichkeiten. Im Inneren der *machiya* genannten schmalen und engen Stadthäuser Kyotos aus dem 19. Jahrhundert beschwören natürliches Sonnenlicht, handgefertigte Bambus-Jalousien und mit *shoji*-Papier bespannte Stellschirme sogar die Illusion eines naturnahen Lebens herauf. Herbstnebel verschleiern das strohgedeckte

The Five Elements, building blocks of Japanese style, are evident not only in traditional homes, but also in the most contemporary designs by such architects as Tadao Ando and Kengo Kuma, whose Lotus House is an exhilarating composition of white travertine stone, polished hardwood, water, and air.

Long before the words "eco-friendly" made their way into everyday language in Western society, the Japanese were utilizing and recycling natural materials, an impulse that's evident in contemporary buildings like the home of architect Yoshihiro Takishita, who has dedicated his career to saving historic Japanese *minka* farmhouses like the one he lives in. The *minkas* were built with interlocking pieces by master carpenters using joinery, no nails. When Takishita finds an endangered house, he has it disassembled, packed, moved, and rebuilt. Which begs the questions: along with "green" architecture, did the Japanese invent the prefab, too?

japonaise, se retrouvent non seulement dans les demeures traditionnelles mais aussi dans les projets les plus modernes d'architectes tels que Tadao Ando et Kengo Kuma, dont la « Lotus House » est une composition exaltante de travertin blanc, de bois poli, d'eau et d'air.

Longtemps avant que s'impose le concept du « respect de l'environnement », les Japonais utilisaient et recyclaient des matériaux naturels, une démarche que l'on retrouve dans les bâtiments contemporains tels que la maison de l'architecte Yoshihiro Takishita, qui a consacré sa carrière à sauver des fermes minka *traditionnelles comme celle dans laquelle il vit. Les* minka *étaient construites par des maîtres charpentiers en emboîtant des éléments et sans utiliser un seul clou. Quand Takishita découvre une structure en danger, il la fait démonter, emballer, déplacer et reconstruire ailleurs. Ce qui soulève une autre question : outre l'architecture « verte », les Japonais auraient-ils également inventé le préfabriqué ?*

Dach des 200 Jahre alten japanischen Bauernhauses von Alex Kerr, das der Schriftsteller durch im Boden eingelassene Feuerstellen mit Holz beheizt. Die Bauweise nach der japanischen Fünf-Elemente-Lehre findet sich nicht nur in traditionellen Bauwerken, sondern auch in den Entwürfen zeitgenössischer Architekten wie Tadao Ando und Kengo Kuma, dessen »Lotus House« eine erfrischend-heitere Komposition aus hellem Travertin, poliertem Hartholz, Wasser und Luft darstellt.

Lange bevor das Wort »umweltfreundlich« Eingang ins Lexikon fand, benutzten und recycelten die Japaner natürliche Materialien, ein Impuls, der sich vor allem im Heim des Architekten Yoshihiro Takishita abzeichnet, der sein Arbeitsleben der Rettung historischer *minka*-Bauernhäuser gewidmet hat, wie er selbst eines bewohnt. Die *minkas* wurden aus ineinandergreifenden Holzteilen nach traditioneller Handwerkskunst ohne einen einzigen Nagel zusammengefügt. Wenn Takishita ein gefährdetes Haus findet, lässt er es auseinandernehmen, verpacken, abtransportieren und wieder aufbauen. Was für uns die Frage aufwirft: Haben die Japaner neben der »grünen« Architektur auch die Fertigbauweise erfunden?

"…I live peacefully in a grass hut. Clouds are my best neighbors. Free, so free, day after day. I never want to leave!…"

Ryokan, poet (1758–1831)

«…Je vis paisiblement dans une hutte d'herbe. Les nuages sont mes meilleurs voisins. Libre, si libre, jour après jour. Je ne veux plus partir…»

Ryokan, poète (1758–1831)

»…Friedvoll in einer Hütte aus Gras lebe ich. Meine Nachbarn sind die Wolken. Frei bin ich, so frei, Tag für Tag. Ich will nie wieder fort…«

Ryokan, Dichter (1758–1831)

EXTERIORS

Extérieurs   Aussichten

10/11 Vivid autumnal foliage at Tenmangu Shrine. *Les couleurs vives du feuillage d'automne devant le temple Tenmangu.* Bunt gefärbtes Herbstlaub in den Gärten der Tenmangu-Schreinanlage.

12/13 Tenmangu's *torii* gate and Edo stone lanterns. *Le portail torii et les lanternes Edo en pierre de Tenmagu.* Das *torii*-Tor und Steinlaternen aus der Edo-Zeit, Tenmangu.

14/15 Fall mist over Chiiori, Alex Kerr's farmhouse on Shikoku. *Brumes d'automne sur Chiiori, la ferme d'Alex Kerr à Shikoku.* Herbstnebel über Chiiori, Alex Kerrs Bauernhaus auf Shikoku.

16/17 Exterior of the Dream House, by Belgrade artist Marina Abramović. *La « Dream House » de l'artiste Marina Abramović, originaire de Belgrade.* Außenansicht des »Dream House« der Belgrader Künstlerin Marina Abramović.

18/19 Yoshida Sanso, a former prince's estate in Kyoto. *Yoshida Sanso, un ancien domaine princier à Kyoto.* Yoshida Sanso, das ehemalige Anwesen eines Prinzen in Kyoto.

20/21 Tea for two on the terrace of the Yoshida Sanso guest house. *Thé pour deux sur la terrasse de la maison d'hôtes, Yoshida Sanso.* Tea for two auf der Terrasse des Gästehauses Yoshida Sanso.

22/23 The serenity of a Kyoto interior garden, Tawaraya. *La sérénité d'un jardin intérieur à Tawaraya, Kyoto.* Die friedvolle Ruhe eines Innengartens im Tawaraya in Kyoto.

24/25 The skylit entry to the Sugimoto House in Kyoto. *L'entrée protégée d'une verrière de la maison des Sugimoto à Kyoto.* Der durch ein schlichtes Oberlicht erhellte Eingangsbereich des »Sugimoto I Iouse« in Kyoto.

26/27 Twin guardians flank the entrance to Yoshihiro Takishita's house in Kamakura. *Deux gardiens de pierre flanquent l'entrée de la maison de Yoshihiro Takishita à Kamakura.* Wächterstatuen flankieren den Zugang zu Yoshihiro Takishitas Haus in Kamakura.

28/29 The monk Issho meditates in the woods at Chizanso Villa. *Le moine Issho médite dans la forêt de la villa Chizanso.* Der Mönch Issho meditiert im Wald der Villa Chizanso.

30/31 Edo stone lantern in woods surrounding Chizanso Villa. *Une lanterne Edo en pierre dans la forêt qui entoure la villa Chizanso.* Steinlaterne aus der Edo-Zeit im Bambuswald der Villa Chizanso.

32/33 Afternoon light bathes the Bodhisattva Hall, Chizanso Villa. *La lumière de l'après-midi baigne le hall du Bodhisattva, villa Chizanso.* Die Bodhisattva-Halle in der Villa Chizanso ist in nachmittägliches Licht getaucht.

34/35 The Hoshi River rushes through Hoshi-no-yu Onsen in Gunma. *Le Hoshi gargouille au milieu de Hoshi-no-yu Onsen à Gunma.* Der Fluss Hoshi strömt durch den Hoshi-no-yu Onsen in Gunma.

36/37 A tiny bridge crosses Hoshi Onsen's famous hot springs. *Un petit pont enjambe les célèbres sources chaudes de Hoshi Onsen.* Eine überdachte Brücke überquert den Fluss bei den berühmten heißen Quellen von Hoshi Onsen.

38/39 Entrance to the Yasaka Jinja Shrine in the Gion District of Kyoto. *L'entrée du temple Yasaka Jinja dans le Gion District de Kyoto.* Eingang zum Yasaka-Jinja-Schrein im Gion-Viertel von Kyoto.

40/41 Floating elegance: The House of Light by James Turrell, in Tokamachi, Niigata. *Elégance flottante : la « House of Light », à Tokamachi, Niigata.* Schwebende Eleganz: das »House of Light« von James Turrell in Tokamachi, Niigata.

42/43 A rose-colored glow bathes the exterior wall of the House of Light. *Une lueur rosée baigne le mur extérieur de la « House of Light ».* Die Außenmauer des »House of Light« rosa-farben erleuchtet.

44/45 Tadao Ando's Benesse House at the Art Site in Naoshima. *« Benesse House », de Tadao Ando, sur le site d'art contemporain de Naoshima.* Tadao Andos »Benesse House«, Art Site Naoshima.

46/47 At Kengo Kuma's Lotus House travertine block screens define the space. *Dans la « Lotus House » de Kengo Kuma, des écrans en panneaux de travertin définissent l'espace.* Travertin-Steinblöcke definieren den Raum in Kengo Kumas »Lotus House«.

48/49 Kuma's Forest Floor house in Nagano appears almost weightless. *La maison « Forest Floor » de Kuma à Nagano semble presque en état d'apesanteur.* Kumas »Forest Floor«-Haus in Nagano wirkt nahezu schwerelos.

50/51 Tokyo's lush Ueno Park is an urban oasis. *Le luxuriant parc Ueno constitue une oasis au cœur de Tokyo.* Der üppige Ueno-Park in Tokio ist eine städtische Oase.

52/53 Tokyo's robot-like Hotel Sofitel is a Ueno landmark. *L'hôtel Sofitel de Tokyo se dresse tel un robot dans le parc Ueno.* Tokios roboterähnliches Hotel Sofitel ist ein Wahrzeichen des Ueno-Viertels.

54/55 Urban buzz: A bird's-eye view of Tokyo's bustling Shinjuku district. *Brouhaha urbain : une vue aérienne du quartier affairé de Shinjuku à Tokyo.* Großstadtpanorama: ein Blick aus der Vogelperspektive über Tokios geschäftigem Shinjuku-Bezirk.

"...Autumn approaches, and the heart begins to dream. Of four-tatami rooms..."

Basho, poet (1644–1694)

« ...L'automne approche et le cœur se met à rêver. De pièces à quatre tatamis ...»

Basho, poète (1644–1694)

»...Der Herbst kommt und das Herz beginnt zu träumen von Zimmern mit vier tatami ...«

Basho, Dichter (1644–1694)

INTERIORS

Intérieurs   Einsichten

MIX
FRESH MILK
FROM
THE BREAST
WITH
FRESH MILK
FROM
THE SPERM
DRINK
ON
EARTHQUAKE
NIGHTS

WASH YOUR
BEDSHEETS
IN
LEMON JUICE
COV
THE PILLOW
WITH
GREEN
LEAVES

ON YOUR
KNEES,
CLEAN
FLOOR
WITH YOU
BREATH
INHALE
DUS

IN TIME OF
DOUBT
KEEP A SMALL
METEORITE

YOUR
MOUTH

RUN
IN THE
RAINBOW
DIRECTION

SCREMiG

60/61 Rice-paper lamps and a scroll decorate Yoshida Sanso's main hall. *Des lampes en papier de riz et un kakémono décorent la salle principale de Yoshida Sanso.* Lampen aus Reispapier und ein Rollbild schmücken den Hauptraum des Gästehauses Yoshida Sanso.

62/63 A *tatami* room prepared for sleeping, Yoshida Sanso. *Une pièce tapissée d'un tatami est préparée pour la nuit, Yoshida Sanso.* Ein mit *tatami*-Matten ausgelegtes Zimmer, vorbereitet zum Schlafen, Yoshida Sanso.

64/65 A western-style wooden jalousie over *shoji* screens, Yoshida Sanso. *Une jalousie en bois à l'occidentale au-dessus d'écrans shôji, Yoshida Sanso.* Holzjalousie im westlichen Stil über mit *shoji*-Papier bespannten Schiebetüren, Yoshida Sanso.

66/67 Arts-and-crafts-style lamp atop a traditional Japanese low table. *Une lampe de style Arts and crafts posée sur une table basse traditionnelle.* Eine Lampe im Stil der Arts-and-Crafts-Bewegung auf einem niedrigen Tisch im traditionellen japanischen Stil.

68/69 Nature, enclosed: One of Tawaraya's "bubble gardens," Kyoto. *La nature, cloîtrée : un des « jardins bulles » de Tawaraya.* Eingeschlossene Natur: einer der »Bubble«-Gärten im Tawaraya, Kyoto.

70/71 Chinese scrolls and hardwood table in Alex Kerr's living room in Tenmangu. *Des rouleaux chinois et une table en bois dur dans le séjour d'Alex Kerr à Tenmangu.* Chinesische Rollbilder und ein Holztisch in Alex Kerrs Wohnzimmer im Tenmangu-Schreingelände.

72/73 Building a fire over sunken hearths at the Chiiori farmhouse. *La préparation du feu dans des foyers creusés dans le sol dans une ferme à Chiiori.* Feuer machen: im Boden eingelassene Feuerstelle im Chiiori-Bauernhaus.

74/75 Calligraphy at Chiiori: The Japanese character for "spear." *Calligraphie à Chiiori : le caractère japonais pour « lance ».* Kalligrafie im Chiiori-Bauernhaus: das japanische Schriftzeichen für »Speer«.

76/77 Weathered beams at Chiiori. The farmhouse was built without nails. *Des poutres patinées par le temps à Chiiori. La structure est construite sans un seul clou.* Verwitterte Balken im Chiiori-Bauernhaus, das ohne jeden Nagel gebaut wurde.

78/79 Walking in the Zen meditation room at the Chizanso Villa. *Déambulation dans la salle de méditation zen de la villa Chizanso.* Im Zen-Meditationsraum der Villa Chizanso.

80/81 At the Dream House: Slogans by conceptual artist Marina Abramović. *Dans la « Dream House » : des slogans de l'artiste conceptuelle Abramović.* Im »Dream House«: Leitsprüche der Konzept-Künstlerin Marina Abramović.

82/83 Guests at the Dream House wear custom-made "dream suits." *Pour visiter la « Dream House » il faut revêtir des « combinaisons pour rêver ».* Die Gäste im »Dream House« tragen die dort üblichen »Traumanzüge«.

84/85 Dream House guests arrive and enter by the "Explanation Room." *On entre dans la « Dream House » par la « salle des explications ». Gäste betreten das »Dream House« durch den »Explanation Room«.*

86/87 Old-fashioned brick hearth in kitchen, Sugimoto House, Kyoto. *Un vieux four en pierre dans la cuisine de la maison des Sugimoto, Kyoto. Ein altmodischer Ziegelherd in der Küche des »Sugimoto House«, Kyoto.*

88/89 Traditional iron kettle for making green tea, Sugimoto House, Kyoto. *Une théière en fonte traditionnelle pour le thé vert, maison des Sugimoto, Kyoto. Traditionelle eiserne Teekanne zur Zubereitung von grünem Tee, »Sugimoto House«, Kyoto.*

90/91 Simplicity and functionality: *Tatami* sleeping room, Nishioshikoji-cho, Kyoto. *Simplicité et fonctionnalité : une chambre tapissée d'un tatami préparée pour la nuit, Nishioshikoji-cho, Kyoto. Schlicht und funktional: tatami-Schlafzimmer, Nishioshikoji-cho, Kyoto.*

92/93 Gold handpainted Edo folding screen, Nishioshikoji-cho. *Un paravent doré peint à la main de l'époque Edo, Nishioshikoji-cho. Goldfarbener, handbemalter Stellschirm aus der Edo-Zeit, Nishioshikoji-cho.*

94/95 Wild iris in front of a *shoji* rice-paper window, Nishirokkaku-cho, Kyoto. *Un iris sauvage devant une fenêtre shôji en papier de riz, Nishirokkaku-cho, Kyoto. Die Silhouette einer wilden Iris vor einem mit shoji-Reispapier bespanntem Fenster, Nishirokkaku-cho, Kyoto.*

96/97 Edo-period wooden folding screens in the bedroom, Nishirokkaku-cho. *Panneaux coulissants en bois de l'époque Edo dans une chambre de Nishirokkaku-cho. Holzgeschnitzte Stellschirme aus der Edo-Zeit in einem Schlafzimmer in Nishirokkaku-cho.*

98/99 Sunlight streams through slatted windows, Nishirokkaku-cho. *La lumière du soleil se déverse à travers les fentes des fenêtres, Nishirokkaku-cho. Sonnenlicht strömt durch Fensterschlitze in Nishirokkaku-cho.*

100/101 Paper lanterns by Isamu Noguchi at Masatoshi Izumi's Stone House. *Une lanterne en papier d'Isamu Noguchi dans la « Stone House » de Masatoshi Izumi. Papierlaterne von Isamu Noguchi in Masatoshi Izumis »Stone House«.*

102/103 Metal, earth: Granite walls and steel-trussed ceiling, Stone House, Kagawa. *La terre et le métal : des murs en granit et des poutrelles en acier dans la « Stone House », Kagawa. Wände aus Granit und Decke mit Stahlkonstruktion im »Stone House«, Kagawa.*

104/105 Meiji-inspired arched windows over hot springs. *Des fenêtres cintrées inspirées par le style de la période Meiji dominent des bassins alimentés par des sources d'eau chaude. Von der Meiji-Zeit inspirierte Bogenfenster über den Thermalbecken.*

106/107 Wooden benches and floors in the washing area, Hoshi-no-yu, Gunma. *Des bancs et des sols en bois dans le coin où l'on se lave, Hoshi-no-yu, Gunma. Holzbänke und -böden im Badebereich, Hoshi-no-yu, Gunma.*

108/109 Relaxing view from guest room at Hoshi Onsen. *Une chambre d'hôte d'Hoshi Onsen à la vue apaisante.* Ein entspannender Blick aus dem Fenster eines Gästezimmers in Hoshi Onsen.

110/111 Sliding screens allow House of Light guests to sleep "alfresco." *Grâce aux parois coulissantes, les clients de la « House of Light » peuvent dormir à la belle étoile.* Schiebetüren erlauben den Gästen im »House of Light«, wie im Freien zu schlafen.

112/113 Wooden washbucket and stool at the bathing area, House of Light. *Un seau et un tabouret en bois au bord du bassin des ablutions, « House of Light ».* Hölzerner Schöpfeimer und Hocker im Badehaus des »House of Light«.

114/115 Balinese wooden table and benches in the open-plan living room of the Lotus House. *Dans le séjour ouvert de la « Lotus House », une table et des bancs en bois balinais.* Holztisch und Bänke aus Bali im offenen Wohnbereich des »Lotus House«.

116/117 Afternoon light illuminates the music room, Kengo Kuma's Lotus House. *Le salon de musique de la « Lotus House » de Kengo Kuma, inondé par la lumière de l'après-midi.* Das Musikzimmer in Kengo Kumas »Lotus House« ist in nachmittägliches Licht getaucht.

118/119 An inside and outside bath (*rotenburo*) at Kuma's Lotus House. *Un bain intérieur et extérieur (rotenburo) dans la « Lotus House » de Kuma.* Eine Innen- und eine Außenwanne (*rotenburo*) in Kumas »Lotus House«.

120/121 Kengo Kuma's Forest Floor has a transparent living room. *Le séjour transparent de la maison « Forest Floor » de Kengo Kuma.* Kengo Kumas »Forest Floor«-Haus hat ein transparentes Wohnzimmer.

122/123 Ground-floor *tatami* gallery, with a painted paravent, Yoshihiro Takishita. *Au rez-de-chaussée, une galerie tapissée de tatamis, Yoshihiro Takishita.* *Tatami*-Galerie im Erdgeschoss, an der Wand ein bemalter Stellschirm, Yoshihiro Takishita.

124/125 Reed mats tethered to timbers shelter Takishita's reading room. *Des nattes en roseaux attachées aux poutres protègent la bibliothèque de Takishita.* An den Holzbalken des Dachstuhls befestigte Schilfmatten in Takishitas Lesezimmer.

126/127 A Western-style fireplace warms Takishita's sitting room. *Une cheminée à l'occidentale chauffe le séjour des Takishita.* Ein Kamin im westlichen Stil spendet Wärme: Takishitas Wohnzimmer.

128/129 Recessed bookshelves and natural light, in Yoshifumi Nakamura's house. *Une bibliothèque encastrée et la lumière naturelle dans la maison de Yoshifumi Nakamura.* Eingebaute Bücherregale und natürliches Licht in Yoshifumi Nakamuras Haus.

130/131 A brown leather daybed tucked into a recess at the Nakamura House, Tokyo. *Un lit de repos en cuir brun dans une alcôve de la maison des Nakamura, Tokyo.* Eine Chaise-longue aus braunem Leder in einer Wandnische in Nakamuras Haus in Tokio.

132/133 Handmade wooden cabinets and an iron woodburning stove, Nakamura House. *Des placards artisanaux et un poêle à bois, maison des Nakamura.* Handgefertigte Holzschränke und ein eiserner Holzofen in Nakamuras Haus.

134/135 Dining at sunset in Tadao Ando's 4x4 House, Akashi, Hyogo. *La splendeur du coucher de soleil devant un verre de saké dans la « 4x4 House » de Tadao Ando, Akashi, Hyogo.* Abendlicht der untergehenden Sonne in Tadao Andos »4x4 House«, Akashi, Hyogo.

"…Everything is sculpture. Any material, any idea born without hindrance into space, I consider sculpture…"

Isamu Noguchi, sculptor (1904–1988)

«…Tout est sculpture. Toute matière, toute idée née dans l'espace sans entrave m'apparaissent comme des sculptures…»

Isamu Noguchi, sculpteur (1904–1988)

»… Alles ist Skulptur. Stoffliches und Unstoffliches, jede frei in den Raum gesetzte und in ihn ausstrahlende Materie oder Idee betrachte ich als Skulptur …«

Isamu Noguchi, Bildhauer (1904–1988)

DETAILS
Détails   Details

夢の家

Dream House

Marina Abramovic

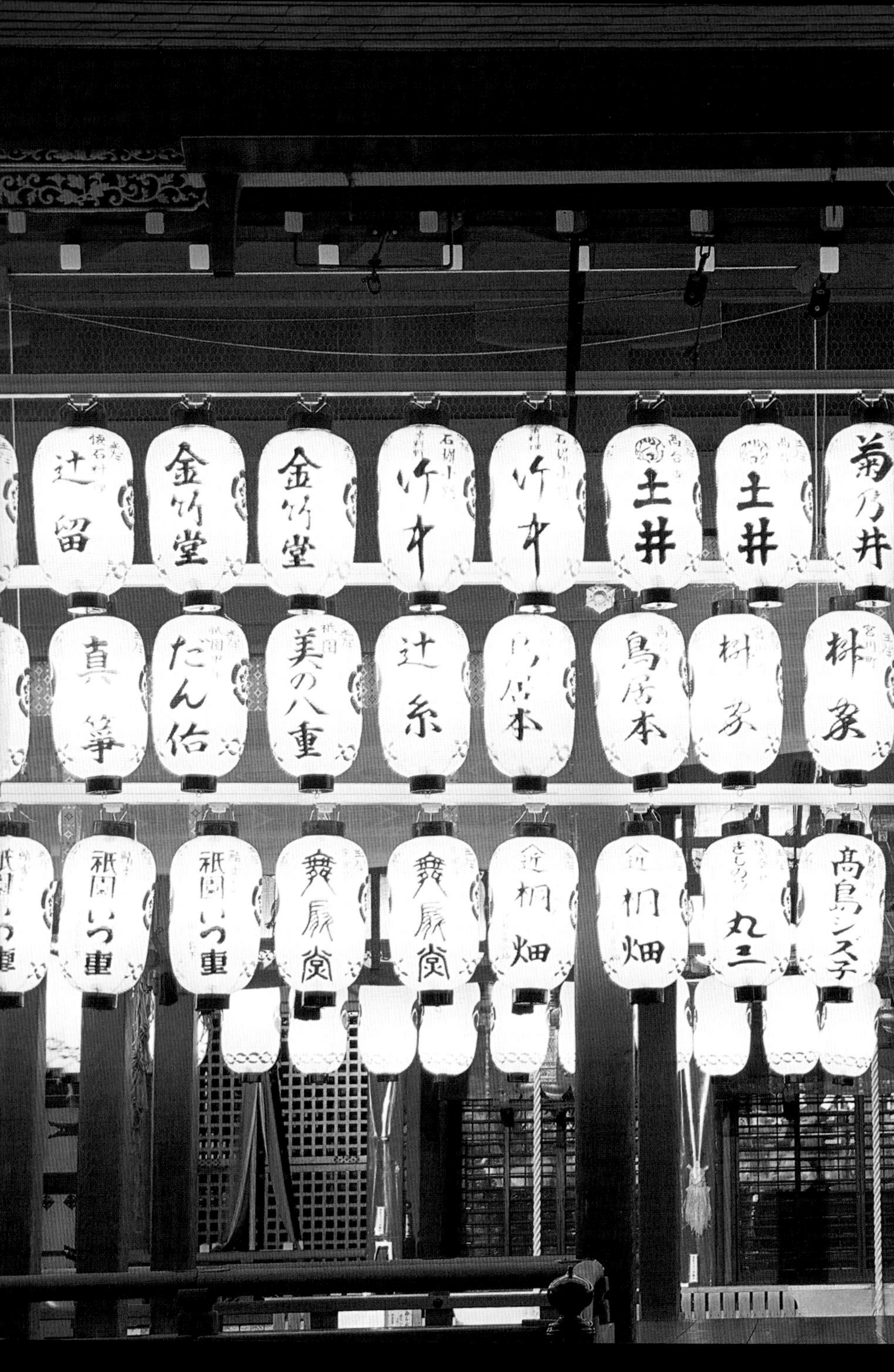

辻留
金竹堂
金竹堂
土井
土井
菊乃井
真箏
美の八重
辻糸
鳥居本
祇園いつ重
祇園いつ重
舞扇堂
舞扇堂
桐畑
桐畑
丸三
高島シズ子

142 Kyoko Nakamura, daughter Tomoko, proprietors of Yoshida Sanso. *Kyoko Nakamura et sa fille Tomoko, les propriétaires de Yoshida Sanso.* Kyoko Nakamura mit ihrer Tochter Tomoko, die Eigentümerinnen des Gästehauses Yoshida Sanso.

144 Antique farming implements at Chiiori farm. *De vieux outils agricoles dans une ferme de Chiiori.* Antikes bäuerliches Arbeitsgerät, Chiiori.

145 Old roof tiles imprinted with *mon* (family crests), Chiiori. *Des tuiles anciennes avec des dessins mon (armoiries) entreposées à Chiiori.* Zwischengelagerte antike Dachziegeln mit japanischen Familienwappen *(mon)*, Chiiori.

146 Samurai triple oak leaf crest, Chiiori. *Un blason de samourai à trois feuilles de chêne à Chiiori.* Samurai-Wappen in Form von drei stilisierten Eichenblättern, Chiiori.

148 Edo-era stone lanterns at Tenmangu. *Lanternes en pierre de l'époque Edo à Tenmangu.* Steinlaternen aus der Edo-Zeit in den Gärten der Tenmangu-Schreinanlage.

149 Mossy old stone lanterns in the garden of the Stone House. *De vieilles lanternes en pierre envahies de mousse près de « Stone House ».* Bemooste alte Steinlaternen im Garten des »Stone House«.

150 Gold-lacquered soup bowl, glass of rice wine, Yoshida Sanso. *Des bols de soupe laqués or et un verre d'alcool de riz, Yoshida Sanso.* Goldlackierte Suppenschüssel und ein Glas Reiswein im Yoshida Sanso.

152 Straw slippers to walk on *tatami* floors, Yoshida Sanso. *Des pantoufles en paille pour marcher sur les* tatamis, *Yoshida Sanso.* Nur mit Hauspantoffeln aus Stroh betritt man die *tatami*-Böden im Yoshida Sanso.

153 Bronze lantern with lotus motif, Sugimoto House. *Une lanterne en bronze couronnée d'un lotus, « Sugimoto House ».* Bronzelaterne mit Lotusmotiv, »Sugimoto House«.

154 Stained-glass transom with prince's crest, Yoshida Sanso. *Un vitrail avec des armoiries princières, Yoshida Sanso.* Oberlicht aus farbigem Glas mit Prinzen-Wappen, Yoshida Sanso.

156 Bedtime reading: Calligraphy by Shina-gawa, the late owner of Yoshida Sanso. *Livre de chevet : de la calligraphie de Shina-gawa, ancien proprié-taire de Yoshida Sanso.* Bettlektüre: Kalligrafie von Shinagawa, ver-storbener Besitzer von Yoshida Sanso.

157 A flower arrangement on a black lacquer desk, Yoshida Sanso. *Une composition florale sur un bureau en laque noire, Yoshida Sanso.* Ein schwarzer Lack-schreibtisch mit einem Blumenarrangement, Yoshida Sanso.

158 Bright red mail-box and welcome lantern, Hoshi Onsen. *Une boîte aux lettres rouge vif et une lanterne souhaitant la bienvenue, Hoshi Onsen.* Knallroter Briefkasten und Willkommens-Laterne, Hoshi Onsen.

160 Entry plaque welcomes guests to the Dream House. *Une plaque accueille les visiteurs à la « Dream House ».* Die Tafel am Eingang heißt die Gäste im »Dream House« willkommen.

161 At the Dream House, guests may use the "telepathy telephone." *À la « Dream House », les visiteurs peuvent utiliser le « téléphone télépathique ».* Im »Dream House« dürfen die Gäste das »Telepathie-Telefon« benutzen.

162 Hanging banner with crest, Sugimoto House, Kyoto. *Une bannière ornée d'armoiries à la « Sugimoto House », Kyoto.* Banner mit Wappen im »Sugimo-to House«, Kyoto.

164 The outer gate of the shrine at Tenmangu. *Le portail du temple de Tenmangu.* Das äußere Tor der Tenmangu-Schreinanlage.

165 A Buddhist monk is the caretaker of Chizanso Villa. *Le régisseur de la villa Chizanso est un moine bouddhiste.* Ein buddhistischer Mönch ist der Hauswart der Villa Chizanso.

166 Wooden buckets for washing before entering the bath at Hoshi Onsen. *Des baquets pour se laver avant d'entrer dans les bassins à Hoshi Onsen.* Holzbottiche zum Waschen vor dem Badehaus in Hoshi Onsen.

168 A tall wooden soaking tub for guests of the Dream House. *Une haute baignoire en bois à la « Dream House ».* Ein großer hölzerner Badezuber für die Gäste im »Dream House«.

169 Flat-topped rice farmer's straw hats, Hoshi Onsen. *Des chapeaux de paille de paysans, Hoshi Onsen.* Flache Bauernhüte aus Reisstroh, Hoshi Onsen.

170 Hallway at Izumi's Stone House, lit by a Noguchi paper lantern. *Couloir de la « Stone House » d'Izumi, éclairé par une lanterne en papier de Noguchi.* Eingangsbereich im »Stone House« von Izumi mit Papierlaterne von Noguchi.

172 Antique wrapped box, Chizanso Villa. *Une boîte ancienne enveloppée dans un balluchon, villa Chizanso.* Antike, verpackte Kiste, Villa Chizanso.

173 Box containing tea ceremony utensils, Chizanso Villa. *Un coffret contenant les ustensiles de la cérémonie du thé, villa Chizanso.* Eine Kiste mit den Utensilien für die Teezeremonie, Villa Chizanso.

174 Burst of spring: Peony blossom in handwoven basket, Nishioshikoji-cho. *Une touche de printemps : une pivoine dans un panier tressé, Nishioshikoji-cho.* Frühlingsbeginn: Pfingstrosenblüte in einem geflochtenen Korb, Nishioshikoji-cho.

176 Cedar oval soaking tub at the Nakamura House, Tokyo. *Une baignoire ovale en cèdre dans la maison des Nakamura, Tokyo.* Ovaler Badezuber aus Zedernholz im Haus von Nakamura, Tokio.

177 Nakamura's library features a woven basket and volumes of books. *La bibliothèque des Nakamura : panier tressé et volumes savants.* In Nakamuras Bibliothek sind ein geflochtener Tragekorb und viele Bücher zu sehen.

178 Paper lanterns bearing with Japanese and ancient Chinese calligraphy, Kyoto. *Des lanternes en papier ornées de calligraphies japonaises et chinoises.* Mit japanischen und alten chinesischen Schriftzeichen geschmückte Papierlaternen, Kyoto.

180 Interior of the Claska Hotel in Tokyo. *L'intérieur de l'hôtel Claska, Tokyo.* Im Hotel Claska in Tokio.

181 Red antique boxes add a touch of color to the Nakamura House. *Des boîtes rouges anciennes ajoutent une touche de couleur dans la maison des Nakamura.* Rote antike Kisten verleihen Nakamuras Haus eine farbige Note.

183 Clematis climbing in a bamboo vase, Nishirokkaku-cho, Kyoto. *Une clématite dans un vase en bambou, Nishirokkaku-cho, Kyoto.* Clematisranken in einer Bambusvase, Nishirokkaku-cho, Kyoto.

184 Inside the Oval at Tadao Ando's Benesse House, Naoshima. *À l'intérieur de l'ovale, la « Benesse House » de Tadao Ando à Naoshima.* Im Oval von Tadao Andos »Benesse House«, Naoshima.

185 Mellow mood: Entrance to the bath at "House of Light." *Ambiance sereine : l'entrée du bain de la « House of Light ».* Besinnliches Ambiente: Eingang zum Bad im »House of Light«.

186 Bottles of premium sake, bar, Claska Hotel, Tokyo. *Des bouteilles de saké de qualité supérieure, bar de l'hôtel Claska, Tokyo.* Flaschen mit Premium-Sake in der Bar des Hotels Claska, Tokio.

Living in Japan
Ed. Angelika Taschen / Photos: Reto Guntli / Text: Alex Kerr, Kathy Arlyn Sokol / Hardcover, 200 pp.
€ 19.99 / $ 29.99 / £ 16.99 / ¥ 3,900

The Hotel Book.
Great Escapes Asia
Ed. Angelika Taschen / Text: Christiane Reiter / Hardcover, 400 pp. / € 29.99 / $ 39.99 / £ 24.99 / ¥ 5.900

Inside Asia Vol. II
Ed. Angelika Taschen / Photos: Reto Guntli / Text: Sunil Sethi Hardcover, 448 pp. / € 39.99 / $ 59.99 / £ 29.99 / ¥ 7,900

"Inside Asia is certainly lavish: a two-volume, cloth-bound and gold-edged tour around the Far East's most sumptuous interiors." —*Wallpaper*, London on Inside Asia

" Buy them all and add some pleasure to your life."

60s Fashion
Ed. Jim Heimann
70s Fashion
Ed. Jim Heimann
African Style
Ed. Angelika Taschen
Alchemy & Mysticism
Alexander Roob
Architecture Now!
Ed. Philip Jodidio
Art Now
Eds. Burkhard Riemschneider, Uta Grosenick
Atget's Paris
Ed. Hans Christian Adam
Bamboo Style
Ed. Angelika Taschen
Barcelona, Restaurants & More
Ed. Angelika Taschen
Barcelona, Shops & More
Ed. Angelika Taschen
Ingrid Bergman
Ed. Paul Duncan, Scott Eyman
Berlin Style
Ed. Angelika Taschen
Humphrey Bogart
Ed. Paul Duncan, James Ursini
Marlon Brando
Ed. Paul Duncan, F.X. Feeney
Brussels Style
Ed. Angelika Taschen
Cars of the 70s
Ed. Jim Heimann, Tony Thacker

Charlie Chaplin
Ed. Paul Duncan, David Robinson
China Style
Ed. Angelika Taschen
Christmas
Ed. Jim Heimann, Steven Heller
James Dean
Ed. Paul Duncan, F.X. Feeney
Design Handbook
Charlotte & Peter Fiell
Design for the 21st Century
Eds. Charlotte & Peter Fiell
Design of the 20th Century
Eds. Charlotte & Peter Fiell
Devils
Gilles Néret
Marlene Dietrich
Ed. Paul Duncan, James Ursini
Robert Doisneau
Ed. Jean-Claude Gautrand
East German Design
Ralf Ulrich/Photos: Ernst Hedler
Clint Eastwood
Ed. Paul Duncan, Douglas Keesey
Egypt Style
Ed. Angelika Taschen
Encyclopaedia Anatomica
Ed. Museo La Specola Florence
M.C. Escher
Fashion
Ed. The Kyoto Costume Institute
Fashion Now!
Eds. Terry Jones, Susie Rushton

Fruit
Ed. George Brookshaw, Uta Pellgrü-Gagel
Greta Garbo
Ed. Paul Duncan, David Robinson
HR Giger
HR Giger
Grand Tour
Harry Seidler
Cary Grant
Ed. Paul Duncan, F.X. Feeney
Graphic Design
Eds. Charlotte & Peter Fiell
Greece Style
Ed. Angelika Taschen
Halloween
Ed. Jim Heimann, Steven Heller
Havana Style
Ed. Angelika Taschen
Audrey Hepburn
Ed. Paul Duncan, F.X. Feeney
Katharine Hepburn
Ed. Paul Duncan, Alain Silver
Homo Art
Gilles Néret
Hot Rods
Ed. Coco Shinomiya, Tony Thacker
Grace Kelly
Ed. Paul Duncan, Glenn Hopp
London, Restaurants & More
Ed. Angelika Taschen
London, Shops & More
Ed. Angelika Taschen

London Style
Ed. Angelika Taschen
Marx Brothers
Ed. Paul Duncan, Douglas Keesey
Steve McQueen
Ed. Paul Duncan, Alain Silver
Mexico Style
Ed. Angelika Taschen
Miami Style
Ed. Angelika Taschen
Minimal Style
Ed. Angelika Taschen
Marilyn Monroe
Ed. Paul Duncan, F.X. Feeney
Morocco Style
Ed. Angelika Taschen
New York Style
Ed. Angelika Taschen
Paris Style
Ed. Angelika Taschen
Penguin
Frans Lanting
Pierre et Gilles
Eric Troncy
Provence Style
Ed. Angelika Taschen
Safari Style
Ed. Angelika Taschen
Seaside Style
Ed. Angelika Taschen
Signs
Ed. Julius Wiedeman
South African Style
Ed. Angelika Taschen

Starck
Philippe Starck
Surfing
Ed. Jim Heimann
Sweden Style
Ed. Angelika Taschen
Tattoos
Ed. Henk Schiffmacher
Tokyo Style
Ed. Angelika Taschen
Tuscany Style
Ed. Angelika Taschen
Valentines
Ed. Jim Heimann, Steven Heller
Web Design: Best Studios
Ed. Julius Wiedemann
Web Design: Best Studios 2
Ed. Julius Wiedemann
Web Design: E-Commerce
Ed. Julius Wiedemann
Web Design: Flash Sites
Ed. Julius Wiedemann
Web Design: Music Sites
Ed. Julius Wiedemann
Web Design: Portfolios
Ed. Julius Wiedemann
Orson Welles
Ed. Paul Duncan, F.X. Feeney
Women Artists in the 20th and 21st Century
Ed. Uta Grosenick

ICONS